At Nightfall

India Howell

BookLeaf Publishing

Presentation by *BookLeaf Publishing*

Web: www.bookleafpub.com

E-mail: info@bookleafpub.com

ISBN: 9789357445320

First edition 2022

DEDICATION

For Mummy and Daddy,

for always believing in me.

To Rise and To Fall

Is it possible to feel bloated and hollowed out at the same time?

Like the vastness of the seas and the skies wouldn't be enough to contain you. But you struggle to uncurl your limbs from the corner of the room.

How is it that silence can weigh so heavy on you yet be so comforting?

Something that is craved, sought after, while it wraps its fingers around your throat.

Choking the life out of you while you ask for more.

Where have I gone?

I've lost myself.

Floating somewhere just beyond reach.

A memory just forming, only to scatter away under the light of consciousness.

I long to forget. But also, I work to remember.

To lose oneself implies that you once belonged to yourself. But was I ever truly mine?

Or was I (am I) yet another reincarnation, yet another manifestation, yet another shape in the kaleidoscope of this reality? Is a mirage real simply because we see it? Or is it fake because it's not really there?

Did I lose myself? Or am I simply shifting, like water down a stream.

Water.

Eroding.

Stripping back the layers of what once was, what no longer is.

Flowing back into the larger body of the ocean.

Silence.

Waves.

When glass breaks, which shard is the original piece?

Am I breaking or am I being submerged?

Density rises to the surface to be cleared.

Water.

Cleansing.

If you need to be cleansed, does that imply that you were dirty to begin with?

Shame.

If there are no wrong feelings, no wrong reactions, then why am I being told to shift?

Water.

Does a wave have to be a certain size, a certain shape, a certain height before it must return to be part of the ocean?

Or can it just be, in all its destructive potential?

Can I just be, in all my destructive potential.

What if the heaviness was all part of the plan?

What if the lightness was never the end destination?

How can this be a journey if there is no destination?

How can the past exist if the present is all there is?

How can I be so bloated and so hollowed out all at the same time, all in the same moment.

Parallax

Perception is limited, like trying to gaze at the entire night sky through a pinhole.

When stars die, we don't see that on earth. What we see is the star's past, still shining bright above our heads. A cosmic explosion is taking place and we are none the wiser.

When I die, will anyone in the universe see it? Will I go out in such a spectacular manner?

A rupture of space. A ripping of the fabric of reality. An implosion. An enveloping. A going under.

What is it like to die?

Are you lifted out of your body, carried into another state of being?

Or do you sink, retreating further into yourself, until you've folded yourself so small there's nothing left.

A long walk home on a dark night.

The Dead Don't Sleep

I stand in the middle of the field

guitar in one hand, your mind in the other.

I strum your sinew, your thoughts cascading into the still air.

I ground into your sensations,

feeling you out.

I can sense the reverberations of your quiet breaths in my chest—

goosebumps ripple as your hands ghost over mine

as my fingers get caught

on the ridged surface of your mind.

I strum your guitar

I play your melodies

I sing your songs

as you beat on the earth beneath me.

Hunger

I watch your thoughts dribble out of your ears

and greedily gobble them up.

A liquid breakfast.

I watch you open your eyes wide as your body
comes apart,

flesh peeling away to reveal bruised bone.

A rotten feast.

I crouch naked over your remains, blood
dripping from my chin,

hitting the floor in a sickening rhythm.

Sinking my teeth into the forbidden fruit, I
watch for your reaction.

Do I disgust you? I hope I do.

Fly On The Wall

Trapped in this moment

like an insect in resin.

Will you string me up,

wear me around your neck,

keep me close?

Or will you put me on display,

next to your other specimens

neatly placed in a row,

all facing forwards.

Untitled

My bones crack and fall with the leaves in
autumn,

I bury them quietly under the snow in winter.

My breath still echoes, cushioned by the white
blanket covering the ground,

hollow promises whistling through the hairline
fractures in my skull.

I can just about make out of the gravesite—

shallow, marked by a soft indent in the shape of
my womb.

The husk of my being bursts through the soil and
renews with the chirping of the birds in spring.

I can see flowers – pink and blue and orange –
winding their thin stems around my rib cage.

I bloat and bruise in the summer heat, like the
low-hanging fruit of a poisoned tree.

Would you dare to eat?

I have been told not to.

Walk a Mile

I walk until the streets turn black and my eyes turn red

I walk until the pavement knows me better than you do.

I remember the way you looked at me

as I carefully picked my limbs off the bathroom floor.

You looked at me like I was an open book—

like you couldn't wait to snap my spine

and scribble in the margins of my memories.

I walk until the hedges lining the picture book houses know my name,

until the windows blink back at me

and the doors hang open on their hinges,

spilling my secrets into the night air.

I walk until the paths become quiet

hushed tones blurring into silence.

I play chicken, except in reverse—

wait for hours after a car goes by to cross.

I don't do danger these days

I still have marks from last time.

I couldn't walk today.

You shut me inside,

clipped my wings

and decorated the walls with my cries.

So today I'll sit

and bleed and bleed and bleed,

and tomorrow I'll crawl into the kitchen

on scraped hands and knees

and soak my underwear in milk.

Little Girl Lost

My fourteen-year-old self stares at me with your
eyes—

accusatory, laying blame.

She bleeds from her hands, those hands you held
down.

Her feet are bloodied and blistered from walking
across the hot coals of your rage.

Did she deserve it?

Did she have to die for your sins?

I see her everywhere, just on the edge of my
vision.

She stands behind me in mirrors, Bloody
Mary-style.

I can feel the mattress depress with her weight
when I lay down to sleep,

can feel the walls of my bedroom expand and contract with her shaky breath in the dead of night—

the room where she was forced to grow

against her will, bit by bit,

innocent dreams and naïve trust pulled from her open mouth like a perverse magic trick.

I want to drag her into the light, expose her, get rid of her, crush her under my heel—

but would I be any better than you if I turned my back on her?

She and I have seen too much, experienced too much—

I can't add to that.

Instead, I make room for her in my bed

buy her a new teddy bear

wrap her up in her favourite blanket

(the one with the pink and blue flowers)

and pull her close to my chest.

I rub her back, feel her breathing slow,

and when I know she's asleep, I treat her with
the tenderness she and I both deserve.

Night night,

sleep tight,

hope the bed bugs don't bite.

I Realised We Were Going Nowhere

Nothing can be created or destroyed,

so I take the anger you drove into my skin,

borne from your mother's pain,

and weave it into the love I stitched from my father's sorrow.

I no longer punish myself for your mistakes;

I praise myself for the kindness I extended to you.

The dust of your incinerated heart

fitted a little too well into the cracks of my broken soul,

but that doesn't mean I owe anything to you

or that I should remain when it's clear I've
outstayed my welcome.

Nothing can be created or destroyed,

so our relationship isn't really over,

the same way it never really started.

We were bound from the beginning,

and your essence will remain with me forever.

But that doesn't mean I still want you.

I've pieced my soul back together,

with a lightness I found in your absence,

so I pray you can rekindle the flame that burned
within your chest,

but I won't set myself on fire anymore to help
you do that.

Déjà Vu

When we're about to die,

do you think our future flashes before our eyes
along with our past?

Do you think we'll be able to see

all that could have been, as well as all that once
was.

How can it be that I'm remembering something
that has yet to happen?

How is it that I've already experienced this
moment?

I have memories from the future

that feel as real as those from the past.

They blend together,

a circle with no end or beginning.

Time is not linear—

it is an infinite loop.

I stand at one point,

you at another.

When do you think our paths will cross?

Some part of me already knows—

I’ve yet to meet her.

But when I do,

I know she’ll guide me

straight into your arms.

Autumn Arrived, and Carried Your Heart To Me

I go to bed with a heart full of longing,

a belly full of yearning.

I saw you today and the way the light reflected off your eyes was intoxicating.

Gold flecks radiating in the dying autumn light

complimented the orange leaves that fell to the ground under your feet.

I would try to come up with some grand literary analogy,

but your laughter is poetry enough.

I never thought I'd ever love,

at least not *love* love, the type that keeps you up at night—

but here I am, curling my limbs around my blanket, pretending it's you,

hiding my flaming face from your eyes that shine so bright, I swear their luminance reaches through my curtains.

Or maybe that's the starlight.

Same difference, really.

I feel far too young to say the words *I long for you*

they sound confined to a period of idyllic romance—

long countryside walks, picnics on plaid blankets while we stare at the clouds, our quiet confessions carried away with the wind,

but they feel true,

they feel *right*.

I long for you.

Maybe one day I'll say those words to your face,

but more likely I'll stutter out some form of,

Want to grab a coffee? Or a cup of tea,
anything's fine.

But either way, I hope you can feel my sincerity,

the way I buckle under your gaze,

the way you could have me with a single word.

Window To The Soul

Window to the soul

broken, boarded up.

The lights are on

but nobody's home.

Knocking on the windows

knocking on the doors—

please let me in.

Darkness reigns outside—

I can feel its movements

tapping on the window

creeping under the door.

Isn't it time for some spring cleaning?

Open up the windows,

allow some fresh air in.

You can't stay here forever—

I can help you.

We can sew your soul back together,

find the pieces of it in amongst your belongings.

Sandwiched next to a family photo and a
memory you'd rather forget,

held in the arms of the teddy bear you used to
cuddle

when your parents' arguments got too scary.

We can stick it back together with glitter glue—

fond memories, childhood innocence.

Eyes are the windows to the soul,

so please,

open them.

Let the sunshine in.

I want to see myself

reflected in your irises

I want to see our future

reflected in those windows,

promises bouncing off the glass,

reflected, refracted

taking on their own shapes, their own potential.

We could build a new house

with new windows—

French ones, ones with space to sit in.

We could gaze at the valleys and hills for hours,

letting our souls wander through the grass

feeling the soil beneath our feet

and heaven above our heads

and remember what it is like

to be whole

to be one.

You don't have to be afraid to open your eyes,

I'm right here

getting lost in the way your lashes tangle together

when you finally flutter them open.

I lock our fingers together

stroke the back of your hand with my thumb,

remind you

that there is so much beauty everywhere,

like the flowing of white curtains on a summers evening

or the dark hues of my eyes.

Eyes are the window to the soul;

the soul is the window to love.

Palm to Palm

You lie only a handspan away from me.

I could reach out,

graze my fingertips over your skin

feel the energy pulsing there,

but something within me makes me hesitate.

I treat you delicately instead,

like you're made of glass

or something more impermanent—

a wisp of smoke

gracefully undulating in space,

ready to fade back into nothingness.

I'm scared that if I do touch you

you'll disappear,

and this moment will end.

I'd do anything—

break the laws of time

rip the fabric of reality to shreds

just to exist here forever,

lying next to you.

Feeling your warmth

knowing you're there,

lying just a handspan away from me.

When you wake, you take my hand

crossing the distance effortlessly,

tangling not only our fingers

but our thoughts together.

Your hands get lost in my mind,

teasing out the knots

tying pretty bows in the loose ends,

laying my thoughts out flat

uncomplicated, unambiguous.

How is it that you're able to unravel me like this?

With a simple touch, a simple smile.

I'm convinced you have magic brimming at your fingertips

or maybe it's just love,

and I'm too afraid to admit that something so ordinary,

and yet so spectacular

has been breaking down all the walls I've spent so long building up.

Love Letter

Loving you takes many forms,

so it is not an exaggeration to say

that I love you more and more each day.

Because I see love in your every gesture,

I feel it in the most ordinary things you do.

Love tastes like mint tea,

clasped in mugs between our hands

on those cold winter mornings,

as we stare out at the snow-covered fields after a long walk.

Love smells like burnt pancakes

after we forgot about them,

because you were making me laugh so hard

I couldn't pull enough air into my lungs.

Love feels like the inside of your hoodies,

(the ones I always like to steal)

because they feel so soft against my skin,

reminding me of your delicate touch—

the many nights we spent lying in bed

your fingers tracing lines up and down my thighs.

Love sounds like your quiet breathing

as I look at you while you sleep—

relaxed features, total surrender.

I wonder what you dream about,

if I'm there.

If so, I hope the dream version of me

loves you as fully and completely

as my wakeful self does.

Love looks like your figure from the back

as I observe you from across the room.

The light of the setting sun casts a halo around your head,

lighting up your skin

warming it, praising it for appreciating its shine.

You turn and look back at me,

catch me staring

and a pretty smile plays on your lips

as I wonder,

dear god,

how on earth did I get this lucky?

Long Days Without You

I've been sleeping early and rising late

allowing my body to melt into my bed.

The sheets remind me of you—

comforting, soft, full of warm promises.

I crave you on mornings like these,

but I know I have to be patient.

I see you in everything,

can feel the traces you've left long after you're gone.

Your body heat radiates behind me while I make breakfast,

and I smile to myself as your voice whispers in my ear,

do you want some croissant with that jam?

You've turned me into a lightning rod—

a conductor for your emotions.

I can sense them from miles away,

like it's my cheeks that move when you smile,

or my shoulders that shake when you laugh.

I go on walks just to see the trees

I remember how you taught me their names.

You see that one?

How the ends of the branches are darker?

How they curve upwards, like a candelabra?

Those are ash.

Some days I weep like the willows you're so fond of—

the loneliness gets too much.

Other days I'm as resilient as the blackthorn,

knowing one day soon

I'll be able to hold you in my arms again.

Memories are a poor substitute

for the magnificence of you.

These Aching Bones

I long to ache.

I long to love so much it makes me sad

I long for those pains in my chest,

the shortness of breath,

the trembling hands.

I long for you to break my heart

then tenderly put it back together.

I long for you to turn up at my house just as the
light begins to die,

apologies falling from your lips, my fingers
rising up to catch them.

I long for your strong arms around me,

careful whispers tangling through my hair as you hold me.

I'm sorry.

I long for you to leave me.

I long to pine, to yearn, to obsess.

I long for you to come back to me,

to realise your world starts under my feet,

to realise you long for me and me only.

I long to love so deeply it scares me.

I long to have arguments so loud they shake my bones.

I long to make up so tenderly it melts into my skin.

I long to ache.

I long for you.

Aged Love

Could you put a ring on my finger like the rings on trees? Those rings record their memories, etched into the very core of their being. The summers they've spent swaying in the breeze, the autumns they've spent shedding their leaves. Could you put a ring on my finger like the rings on trees? The rings that signify their age, what they've seen, what they've done. All the food they've made, all the food they've eaten, all the laughter they've been a part of. All the shade they've provided for those seeking cool air, all the shelter they've created for those seeking a home. Could you put a ring on my finger like the rings on trees? Could you do that?

Summer Showers

I love summer showers,

when the rain is falling softly

and the sky is lit up with the golden rays of the sun.

I'm so used to overcast skies and grey clouds when it rains—

to see the summer

so closely blended with the autumn

feels like a wink from god—

like it got bored playing things by the book

and decided to give us a treat.

It feels like the curtain has been pulled back,

ever so slightly,

and we get to see the beauty and light humour

present in all things.

The universe tells us all a joke

and I laugh until my sides hurt.

YHWH

I find god nestled deep within the forest, next to the beetle making its solitary way up the face of a mushroom. I find god winding its way through the long grass, just ahead of the snake, stalking its prey. I find god at the tips of my mother's fingertips as I watch her make bread, marvelling at the way the soft dough yields to her firm touch. I find god under the peel of the tangerine I eat every morning, cold and sweet and full of juice. I find god interwoven with my cat's fur as I comb it away from her delicate body, helping her cool down in the summer heat. I find god high up in the sky, undulating with the clouds, changing form faster than I can make out clear shapes. I find god reverberating around the laughter of children, as they race each other down the hill, little feet catching in the rough surface. I find god in the rings under my father's eyes, after all the late-night shifts he takes on to provide for us. I find god in the slopes of your kind words, climbing up the stems of the 'y's and falling down the curves of the 'p's. I find god down on my knees, hands clasped in prayer, sending out a message of strength and love. I find god in you, I find god in me, I find god everywhere.

www.ingramcontent.com/pod-product-compliance
Lightning Source LLC
Chambersburg PA
CBHW051740130826
49812CB00033B/937
* 9 7 8 9 3 5 7 4 4 5 3 2 0 *